Divine Love Self Healing
The
At Oneness Healing System

Robert G. Fritchie

World Service Institute

Knoxville, Tennessee

Copyright © 2016 Robert G. Fritchie

Disclaimer: The author of this book does not dispense medical advice or prescribe the use of any medical technique as a form of treatment for physical, emotional, spiritual, or medical problems. The intent of the author is only to offer information of a nature to help you in your quest for spiritual, emotional and physical well-being.

In the event you use the information in this book for yourself, which is your constitutional right, the author, publisher, printer and distributors assume no responsibility for your actions.

Library of Congress Control Number: 2016908195
ISBN 978-0-9976905-0-7
Fritchie, Robert G.
Divine Love Self Healing: The At Oneness Healing System
1st edition July 2016
1. Body, Mind, Spirit – Healing - Prayer and Spiritual
2. Body, Mind, Spirit – Healing - Energy
3. Body, Mind, Spirit – Healing - General

Table of Contents

Chapter 1 Are You Stuck?...................................5

My Challenge...6

Chapter 2 Limited Thinking............................12

Chapter 3   Past Lives.....................................16

Chapter 4 Manifestation................................23

Selling a House...25

Manifesting a Conflicting Belief....................26

Manifesting Healthy Relationships.................27

Building Communications............................28

Chapter 5 All About Divine Love 29

Defining Divine Love.....................................29

When Healing Occurs...................................30

Remember Icebergs 35

Natural Sequence of Events..........................36

Three Lessons About Divine Love.................38

What You Can Heal 40

Chapter 6 Understand the At Oneness Healing System...42

Fast versus Slow Healing.............................44

Review of Basic Spiritual Truths....................47

Surrendering to the Creator..........................49

Science Behind Petitions..............................50

Background and Healing Reports...................51

Angels and Beliefs.......................................52

Healing Others...53

Human Energy Layers...................................54

Alignment with the Creator...........................55

Activating Divine Love..................................58

Symptom Return..59

About Other Healing Modalities 59

Chapter 7 At Oneness Healing System (AOHS)...61

Staying Connected to Divine Love 61

Feeling Divine Love..63
Petition Overview...64
The At Oneness Healing System Petitions.......66
    The At Oneness Petition.............................66
    The Lovingness Petition 67
    Simplified Protocol.....................................67
Duration of Protocol Use...............................69
Recap...70
Buts..72
Pop-Up Symptoms...73
Correct Subconscious Resistance to Healing...73
Helping Young Children..................................75
Chapter 8 Deeper Understandings...................77
    The Role of Focus in Petitions 77
Become "At One with the Divine"...................79
Coping with the Environment..........................80
Breathing 81
Chapter 9 Healing a Single Symptom 84
    Harry's First Pair Usage....................................86
    Harry's Second Pair Usage...............................87
    Harry's Third Pair Usage..................................88
    Harry's Further Pair Usage...............................89
    Teachings...89
Chapter 10 Healing Multiple Illnesses 93
    Day One..95
    Day Two..97
    Day Three..97
    Day Four..98
    AOH Summary of Use 101

Chapter 1

Are You Stuck?

Throughout the world, people are suffering. In the United States we are seeing the erosion of the family, of religion, and of social values, as well as an increase in addictions, especially drug and alcohol. Is our entire society disintegrating?

I believe that civilization suffers today because we have separated ourselves from the Creator of the universe, knowingly or unknowingly. To help people become realigned with the Creator is the reason I wrote my previous book, <u>Being at One with the Divine</u>.

The focus of this new book, <u>Divine Love Self Healing</u>, is twofold:

    To reveal the difficulties that some

Divine Love Self Healing

healing-resistive people overcame in using our At Oneness Healing System, and how most of them were able to achieve success, and,

To introduce you to a comprehensive and easy-to-use application of Divine Love healing.

My Challenge

I have learned that people need a deeper understanding of energy healing with Divine Love in order to change their life situations. As we enter midlife, we are told that it is normal to experience declining health. I do not accept this and neither should you!

I am hopeful that you will learn from this book what you need to not only realign yourself with the Divine, but also to improve your overall health and well being.

A key question: Are you willing to make the commitment to finally let go of whatever is troubling you physically, mentally, and/or spiritually? If your answer is "Yes," this book may help you.

I'm simply identifying a choice that you are free to accept or reject. If you accept, it may lead to the re-establishment of your wellness. If you

Are You Stuck?

reject the choice, you may be stuck with your problem for the rest of your life! What will your commitment cost? Your participation time, a change in your approach to life, and possibly a redefinition of your belief systems and life priorities.

What I will explain to you is a profound healing process that, once begun, will help to change your life for the better. Will it correct all of your problems? Maybe, maybe not; that is up to the Creator. What I can tell you is that with our Divine Love healing process, many people have recovered from illness when no other medical solution was feasible.

Why should you believe me? I have spent more than 35 years doing energy healing work with people from over thirty countries, including the U.S. and Canada. Those who have attended my seminars and webinars, and those who have read my books, have amazing stories to tell. Many have totally recovered their health!

To see some examples, read the Healing Reports on the World Service Institute website located at:

http://www.worldserviceinstitute.org

You may wonder whether everyone has had

great healing results. For various reasons, some did not get well. However, after years of teaching, I have learned what often prevents people from fully recovering their health. As we go through this book together, I'll provide some answers and show how to correct problems. Another purpose of this book is to fill in the gaps in understanding Divine Love spiritual healing. Most people are willing to try something new in the hope that it will relieve them of their pain and suffering. However, few people take the time to fully understand what they need to do to get and stay well.

Everyone is responsible for attaining his or her own wellness in working with Divine Love. Your healing is between you and the Creator. I do not promise you results or make claims because the results will always speak for themselves.

When it comes to the topic of energy healing work, or more specifically, spiritual energy healing, some people become afraid because they cannot see the energy that is helping them. In preparation for what is in the following chapters, let me caution that you will learn some things in this book that may stretch and challenge your present belief systems.

When I began this work in 1979, I didn't have the faintest idea what created healing. I did

Are You Stuck?

note that many self-help programs which purported to help people actually fell short because of one of the following factors:

>   The solution involved many years of deep therapy, often at great expense.

>   Many could not afford the required expensive equipment.

>   Either medical procedures were too costly, or there were no proven, risk-free procedures.

>   The solutions offered were physical and/or mental, but lacked a spiritual connection to make them effective.

I've been fortunate to have worked with many doctors and scientists in the United States who were studying and practicing alternative healing. As I moved through the first 10 years of healing work, I tried various techniques with people who came to me for help. Some techniques worked; some did not. There seemed to be nothing that worked all of the time, for everyone.

When I tried to help people using personal healing energy without the support of the Creator, little of a lasting nature happened. It was not until I achieved a complete union with

Divine Love Self Healing

the Creator, able to give up personal control over all healing situations, that real break-throughs came. And come they did!

When I have used the spiritual process explained to you in this book, complete healing occurred in people who had a variety of major illnesses. On the basis of that success, I designed a series of teaching programs designed to blend the spiritual and the scientific. These programs produced results far greater than any other approach I've seen to date.

People have asked if this Process is "New Age" or "Religious Fundamentalist" or whether a "church" membership is required. No, it is simply spiritual truths, presented in a manner you can use.

Now we are at the threshold of our work together. This book offers guidelines for you on a variety of spiritual, mental, and physical issues as part of your "personal get well program." Even if English is not your first language, please read the book anyway; your internal Spirit knows what is being said and will translate the intent to you.

Please allow yourself time to absorb and understand each chapter because each one builds a foundation of understanding for the following chapters.

Are You Stuck?

We recognize that although people throughout the world have various names for the Creator, it is all the same Divine Creator of the universe. We use the word *Creator*, but if you do not favor that, simply substitute a name of your choosing (God, Higher Power, etc.)

Chapter 2

Limited Thinking

What do you believe is needed for successful healing?

When I first began healing work, I often had mixed results. Sometimes people with incurable diseases would become well and sometimes not. In 1982, I began to utilize the Creator's Divine Love in my healing work and noticed that results improved dramatically.

Yet there were many other conditions such as stress, cancer, arthritis, and blood diseases that did not respond to healing, or responded only partially. I searched for many years to find answers to this question:

Why do some people respond rapidly to healing and others do not?

I observed that when people became ill through accidents or chemical poisoning, they usually responded to healing even when they had no particular religious belief system.

I also noticed that it made a difference when the person being helped believed in the Creator (God). I was not able to help people who did not believe in a Divine Creator. That made sense since Divine Love is God's Love. If you don't believe in the Creator, why would you expect God's Love to work in your life?

Sometimes I was only partially able to help people who said that they did believe in the Creator; these partial results did not make sense to me. Was something else going on that I did not understand? I was puzzled about the results obtained

.

Upon examining the results further, I began to realize that healing is dependent upon many conditions. We will explore what they are throughout this book.

These realizations caused me to rethink the entire subject of healing. Over the next several years, tremendous insights were given to me about the true meaning of spiritual healing. Eventually, my old Mind-Body knowledge was replaced with a spiritual awareness. You see, issues of healing are not solved by simply developing sophisticated healing techniques and then selling those techniques to the public.

Divine Love Self Healing

Rather, healing is a reordering of your life to properly realign yourself with the Creator. This is what my book, <u>Being at One with the Divine</u> attempts to communicate. Once you are at One with the Divine (meaning your energy fields are properly aligned), further healing is accomplished more easily and quickly.

In many countries, solutions to health problems are often seen as solely mental or physical events. However, once you accept that healing with Divine Love energy is a *spiritual process*, complete healing becomes possible because Divine Love *is* the most powerful energy force in the universe.

Whether you've had a religious upbringing or not, we all have inherent limitations in our personal belief systems based upon all the ideas to which we have been exposed. For example, the phrase "spiritual truth" has been subjected to many false teachings, such as trance mediums, charlatans and magicians dealing in psychic phenomenon.

Our direct connection to Divine spirituality was lost.

I want to share with you a simple way to acquire clarity about what is s*piritually true* and to free yourself from limited thinking. Say the following Petition *aloud*:

Limited Thinking

"With my Spirit and Divine Love, I send Divine Love throughout my system and focus upon all of the limited thoughts that prevent me from understanding spiritual truth."

"I release these thoughts to the Creator, and ask that the Creator clear my limited thinking, so that I can accept spiritual truth."

Now close your mouth, breathe in deeply and pulse your breath out through your nose once.

Do you feel energy moving through your body? If so, it means that your system is being cleared from limited beliefs. Try this a few times over the period of an hour, then notice how you respond to new ideas.

Chapter 3

Past Lives

The subject of past lives has been, and continues to be, largely a question of belief systems. Many people have avoided discussion of past lives because of fear or religious beliefs. And yet, people in many cultures support the concept of contact from the "other side."

Many ancient cultures openly discuss the idea that man has lived multiple lives in the past. They believe the Soul carries Soul memories from the past that can be accessed in the present life. The value of accessing Soul memories is to be able to find, identify, and correct past life actions that appear in the present life as discordant energy, which interferes with good health.

In my early years of healing work, I knew nothing of past lives, although I can recall my grandparents sitting quietly, discussing their experiences regarding ancestors who had long

Past Lives

ago passed on. However, these discussions were never public and it was only through my questioning them as a child that I learned about their dearly departed. Members of my mother's family who had passed over and who appeared in dreams or other visual images were generally regarded as *ghosts*.

Many individuals I've met believe that contact with dead relatives is both real and possible; I've come to realize that this contact *is* real. What may prevent us from contacting and talking to deceased relatives is superstition, uncertainty, false religious teachings, or fear of public scorn.

There are practitioners who offer instruction to guide you back through *past lives* utilizing a variety of techniques. I have found that this can be a frightening process for groups and is better dealt with in a one-on-one counseling session.

There are, however, positive benefits to be realized: People who have had a difficult life are relieved once they finally understand how their past experiences affect their behavior or health in this lifetime.

I do not teach past life regression in webinars because of the need for privacy. However, when an individual is truly stuck in their healing efforts, I try to help them privately. When I guide them in a past life regression, they can examine why they are having a problem in this life. Then we can work together to release the problem.

I will explain how to easily do past life regression without allowing fear to creep in. Simply ask the person to utilize their internal Spirit and Divine Love, plus a simple petition to work backwards through their life, or lives, until they reach the incident(s) responsible for their current spiritual healing problem. The petition we use is:

"With my internal Spirit and Divine Love, I go backwards in time to the instance or instances that explain my current (*name your problem*) fully."

As an individual does this, he usually gets images (with his eyes closed) of the life situations he was in that account for the current problem. I tell him to observe exactly what it was that he did in that lifetime that is responsible for the current life problem. It is nearly *always* an unloving action from the past that has *separated* his Soul from the Divine. That separation becomes a *Soul debt* carried forward by the Soul into the current lifetime.

He is also encouraged to ask to be shown

specific details that he can then observe dispassionately, like watching a movie. This is possible because Divine Love protects an individual from experiencing any adverse emotional reaction to an otherwise upsetting observation. Therefore, there is nothing to fear from doing a regression. Our regressions are not hypnotic suggestions; you sit in a chair, fully awake.

Another thing I do is encourage a person to ask their own Spirit to *explain the true meaning* of words heard or scenes witnessed, rather than to assume that he clearly understands what that guidance means. For example, you might see a scene where an angry man is beating a woman. You ask what the scene means and you hear back the single word "unlovingness." If you are the man you may think you are disciplining an unfaithful wife, or you are being depicted as a bully for harming her. But what if you are the woman in the scene? Would you think that the beating was being given to make you more loving or something else?

Since in any past life you could be either a man or woman, you need to ask who you are in the scene and what "unlovingness" means to you in that experience. Once you understand what is happening in your "movie," you will know what symptom to use in a petition to clear the ancient energy condition from your Soul in this lifetime.

Finally, I encourage the participant to go back even further in time with their Spirit and Divine Love to be sure that all the scenes responsible for the current complaint have been identified and understood.

When someone is willing to confront the past, be it in this life or in past lives, he is able to use a simple Petition of his own design to release the "Soul debt." Once the ancient cause is acknowledged and released, it is often a surprise to see just how fast one's system responds when using the At Oneness Healing System (AOHS)!

> Such is the power of Divine Love: It involves no fanfare, no emotion, no guilt, no punishment, no rejection, no sense of unworthiness, and no sense of being unloved. In fact, Divine Love leaves a person feeling *totally* loved.

One recent case comes to mind that will serve as a clear example of what I'm talking about.

I received a call from Louis who was suffering from tremendous pain that could not be released with medicine, therapy, or even our At Oneness Healing System Petitions.

Past Lives

When I guided Louis in a past life regression to determine the root cause of his pain, Louis learned that in ancient times he had been like a king, ruling over a large city. This ruler had decided to seize control of a neighboring town to force the inhabitants to follow his dictates. That desire to control was a violation of the free will of the inhabitants. As a result, Louis incurred a "Soul debt" that was playing out in this lifetime.

After we determined that there were no other past life causes for his pain, I suggested that Louis ask the Creator how to remove the Soul debt. Louis was surprised to learn that the Soul debt had been forgiven as soon as he *acknowledged* the ancient scene.

Next I suggested that Louis ask the Creator what should be done to relieve and heal his pain. Again the answer was a surprise: He was told to live in the present as a spiritual person and to stop thinking about all the potential reasons for his pain.

Louis had been spending his days worrying about causes and treatments. Buried in these feelings was a great deal of frustration because he had tried all practical treatments. Since the problem had a spiritual origin, it follows that the Creator's spiritual recommendation was to "cease and desist."

Divine Love Self Healing

The problem corrected itself once my friend stopped trying to rationalize the situation and self-treat the pain.

Past life regression does not apply to all healing situations. We only use it during private consultations to unblock people who remain"stuck" after using Petitions.

Louis's experience serves as an introduction to the next chapter on *manifestation,* which may also be a confusing subject.

Chapter 4

Manifestation

In my early training, I was exposed to several people who were able to manifest objects at will. This was an extreme demonstration that few can do. When you watch someone with an open hand focus his attention on producing an object in that hand, and then the object appears, it is clear that the person in question has a special skill! If you are living your life at a vibratory state that can handle the energy of Divine Love at whatever vibration level is required, then you too may be capable of manifesting solid objects.

Surprisingly, we all have the ability to manifest. *What* you are able to manifest is a function of the vibratory rate of your body.

What you manifest are the thoughts driving your life. By this I mean that when you think, you create energetic thoughts. *Those thoughts can either serve or harm you and/or others.*

Divine Love Self Healing

Here are two examples with names changed to protect privacy:

> Marcella declared, "I can't be helped because I have cancer and I have already tried everything." Marcella had *manifested* such a strong energetic field of resistance that she could not accept that healing was possible even if that healing came from the Creator. Sadly, this is a very common manifestation.

> Mary Ellen confided, "I can't stand my neighbor and I wish he would die." Mary Ellen had *manifested* a field of hatred that separated and insulated her from most of the people in her life. Her manifestation did not reach full strength in a single occurrence, but accumulated over time. Mary Ellen was unsuccessful using Petitions because she chose to continue her behavior.

With modern medicine, I see another type of manifestation appearing in patients. People want to be well, but their mindset is that all their discomfort can be relieved by someone else. In other words, they are not taking responsibility for their own wellness.

The practice of rushing to the medicine cabinet to get relief, rather than taking the time to determine the *root cause* of a problem often results in a *manifested* habit-forming action. Once we have done this long and often enough, it becomes very difficult to change behavior to achieve healing.

Manifested thought can be good if done properly. Unfortunately, many teachers suggest that all life problems can be changed by simply thinking positively. I have learned that this is only partially true. *You cannot wish away mental or physical illness.* Also, you cannot wish away illness if it has an underlying spiritual cause.

Here are more examples of how people have misapplied manifestation:

Selling a House

Christy had been trying to sell her personal residence without a Realtor. She had been told that all she had to do was hold a positive intention and that buyers would be attracted to her because she was enthusiastic and upbeat. Many prospects came to look, but the house remained on the market with no offers! Christy became very anxious because she needed the house sale money to support herself.

A year later, Christy attended one of our webinars where she learned how to correctly work with our Divine Love Petitions; within weeks her house was sold!

What was the difference?

The situation changed as soon as Christy surrendered her problem to the Creator. Her *anxiety* manifestation was dissolved by using AOHS Petitions. She learned that her growing anxiety had been preventing a solution from manifesting.

Prospective home buyers had picked up on her anxiety and mistakenly concluded something was wrong with the house.

Manifesting a Conflicting Belief

Many health practitioners have had problems healing what I consider to be straightforward symptoms. The problem was that they thought (*manifested*) that healing should follow the medical model that they had been taught.

Even when they tried to work with our At Oneness Healing System, they were not successful. In each case, the practitioners had difficulty accepting that we are teaching and applying a *spiritual* process, as opposed to the mental and/or physical process of their training.

As a result of many years of formal medical

training, they had *manifested* an energetic belief system that prevented them from accepting and applying Divine Love, even though they were fully cognizant that Divine Love *is* a spiritual healing energy, the Creator's Love!

Several physicians succeeded in changing their *manifestations* and several did not.

To succeed they had to be willing to change and to allow the Creator to lead the way.

Manifesting Healthy Relationships

Many people believe they will be able to change the behavior of their significant others. I do not agree with this.

In my experience, change only occurs when individuals are willing to change themselves. If you desire that someone else change his or her behavior, you actually create a *manifested illusion* based upon what you *want* to see happen, rather than what *is* happening.

First work on your own self-healing. When complete, you will be able to determine without emotion whether or not you want to tolerate unhealthy relationships in your life. What you will learn is a spiritual truth: You cannot force someone else to change.

Divine Love Self Healing

Building Communications

The best thing you can do is to hold the thought of sending other people Divine Love to help them, without any other intention attached. When you do this, you *manifest* a condition in which you, and the people around you, are able to temporarily see, and truly hear one another, without any distortion in understanding.

As you progress, you can do the spiritual work required to clear yourself. The people around you will also be able to clear themselves should they choose to do so. Here is a simple petition to send Divine Love into a group of people:

> **"With my Spirit and Divine Love, I send Divine Love into the room to help the people there, according to the Creator's will."**

You can do this in your home, in hospitals, in restaurants, in your place of worship, in your place of business, or anywhere you happen to be. It all works!

Chapter 5

All About Divine Love

Defining Divine Love

Many individuals have grown up in unloving homes, not understanding love or Divine Love because they have been conditioned by their limited definitions of personal love. Personal love can be biased by an assortment of emotions, judgments and conditions imposed upon an individual, or imposed by an individual upon others. To understand Divine Love, we must change our own perceptions to increase our understanding.

Recently, someone struggling with a health issue asked me what it's like to spiritually love oneself. This individual was very good at loving other people, but had no understanding of self love.

When you are experiencing spiritual self love: You can forgive yourself, and you fully accept

Divine Love Self Healing

responsibility for all your decisions; you are happy in your present body; you make the effort to care for yourself; and you are willing to accept Divine Love.

Once you have cleared your obstacles to loving the Creator, loving yourself, and loving other people spiritually with Divine Love, you are ready for your own healing. Until that is accomplished, you may remain "stuck."

Learning to love properly is the secret to achieving your finest healing masterpiece... YOU. To make a profound difference in your life, try saying the following statement, followed by a pulsed breath:

"With my internal Spirit, I accept Divine Love and ask that it replace my definition of personal love."

You may need to say this Petition several times before you begin to see how Divine Love really is different from any definition of personal love. You will develop an entirely new outlook on life, one based upon joy and serenity.

When Healing Occurs

Spiritual healing with Divine Love is a profound process that often confounds scientists. Yet, the results are undeniable.

All About Divine Love

When people utilize our Divine Love Petitions, amazing results are achievable!

You may be struggling to heal because you expect that your healing should occur instant-aneously, or according to your intentions. True healing occurs when:

> You are willing to let healing happen according to the Creator's Will, *not* your will.

> You understand and use the At Oneness Healing System (AOHS) correctly, and

> Soul debts are removed through past life regression.

Your spirit and the Creator determine your healing, not your mind, not your ego, and not your preconceived ideas of healing with "I want it right now" expectations.

To better understand this, let's consider the idea of *free will*

.

Many religious texts discuss *free will* as man's right to choose and make decisions without influence from the Creator. A problem occurs when we try to inject our free will into a Petition that is not in accordance with the Creator's Will. If we try to manipulate Divine Love to

31

Divine Love Self Healing

satisfy a personal agenda, we can become stuck and/or healing *is* denied.

Divine Love is a spiritual gift from the Creator that we can use, but not abuse.

What is the solution to aligning our will to the Creator's will? First, ask yourself:

1. If I believe that the Creator is all powerful and can heal me with Divine Love, then why am I seeking alternative healing methods that do not include Divine Love?

2. Do I believe that the Creator makes possible inventions in science, discoveries in medical research, and new medications, or do I believe that mankind is developing all these without the Creator's support?

3. Am I willing to fully turn over my healing to guidance from the Creator, acknowledging that the means, timing, and results are whatever the Creator wants for me?

These are tough questions, especially when someone is confronted with a potentially terminal illness.

All About Divine Love

Here are my answers to those questions:

Seeking alternative healing methods with Divine Love does *not* mean that you must discontinue traditional medical treatment. You should continue medical solutions if they exist where you live; you can apply Divine Love spiritual healing at the same time. I do caution you to avoid trying on your own a lot of alternatives that have not proven effective.

You are still exercising your free will, but you show wisdom by deferring to the Creator for guidance in spiritual healing. There should be no competition between conventional medicine and the At One-ness Healing Sysytem.

We know that physical contact methods which do not correctly utilize Divine Love can produce limited results. Examine very carefully the results that you have observed in yourself or others over an extended time period. If the condition is not completely healed in five days, then the methodology on which you are spend-ing time and money may be merely lessening your symptom, but not fully healing the underlying cause. Divine Love heals completely, provided that you align your free will with the Creator.

Divine Love Self Healing

I personally believe that inventions are supported by Divine guidance; it is the misuse or overuse of many inventions that can create trouble. If you are using the At Oneness Healing System, it is fine if your doctor offers a solution that has side effects. Since you are still aligning your free will with both the doctor and the Creator, Divine Love will usually heal any side effects.

When we are willing to release our free will to the Creator's will for us, whatever the consequences, then we are in the best possible spiritual, mental and physical state for complete healing to occur. Surrendering our free will to the Creator means that we recognize that spiritual guidance is always needed to achieve the best outcome.

Often we pray for something, and when we get what we prayed for, we naturally believe our prayers have been answered. But if we do *not* get what we prayed for, we may believe we have done something wrong and are being punished. What is actually happening is that we get from the Creator what we *need* in that moment, even though we may not yet recognize the value.

All About Divine Love

Remember Icebergs

You may know that 10% of an iceberg floats above the water and 90% is concealed below the water line. The iceberg is a good metaphor for the conscious and the subconscious mind. The conscious mind (the part above water) enables us to address active issues that we think about. However, our conscious mind does not have an awareness of what we have stored in our subconscious mind (the part below water).

The subconscious mind stores and can suppress traumatic memories which we experience as discordant energies that prevent us from being at one with the Divine. Over many years, these events begin to affect us energetically and impede our cellular memory.

With our Petitions you can purge both your conscious mind and your subconscious mind without reliving a traumatic memory. This allows your cells to function properly and restores your well being, according to the Creator's will.

If you are still "stuck," this is the result of Soul energies that only the Creator can release. That is why you must *ask* the Creator directly to explain to you *why* you have the condition, *what* you need to do to release it, and *how long* and *how often* you need to do specific petitions. Sometimes you may need to do a past life regression to get to the underlying spiritual cause.

Natural Sequence of Events

When you go to a physician, he or she may order tests to reach a diagnosis based on your symptoms. Often, a medicine or procedure will be prescribed to help correct the problem or lessen pain. If your condition does not correct over time, additional tests, procedures or surgeries might be recommended. My point is that whatever healing modality you use requires a multi-phase step-by-step approach that takes time.

Similarly, to use the At Oneness Healing System effectively, it is important for you to proceed slowly and follow the guidelines set forth in this book. When you don't get immediate results, relax; you are doing nothing wrong with respect to Petitions. It is important that you recognize both the need for a behavior change, and the need to implement that change for Petitions to have a lasting effect. For example:

> If you are overweight, you can use Petitions to break a food addiction, but you must also become responsible for

eating nutritionally good food in the correct amounts. Professional nutritionists often recommend that you eliminate sugars, white flour and/or trans fats from your diet.

If you have a bad heart, you might use Petitions to heal your heart, but you may also need to change how you live your life by reducing *stress* and any *unlovingness* that you exhibit toward the Creator, yourself or other people. Anger, hatred, prejudice, and unloving actions are not heart healthy.

If you have chronic pain, you can use Petitions to clear the cause of the pain and the pain itself. If the pain is caused by an accident, your Divine Love healing is generally immediate and lasting. However, if the pain is caused by an emotional upset, it would be wise to examine all aspects of your life, then rid yourself of the causes of your emotional turmoil by using Petitions to avoid re-contaminating yourself. This may translate into a job change, a lifestyle change, or dealing with a personal relationship that has become toxic.

If you experience slow healing, remember that all symptomatic problems in your life are

Divine Love Self Healing

valid feed-back from your body that something needs to be addressed in your Soul, mind, or body; your problems are *not* a punishment.

Divine Love healing can be utilized to heal unloving attitudes and behaviors in your life. We teach you how to do this on the webinars and in this book, but to achieve desirable results, it is up to you to use the Petitions correctly and consistently.

Three Lessons About Divine Love

I know of three people who experienced difficulties in their lives and were unable to use Divine Love completely because of their ingrained limited belief systems. My purpose in discussing these three cases is not to frighten you, but to wake you up! It is time for you to take action in your life to avoid continued discomfort and possible shortening of your life.

In the first case a man did healing work directly on other people using his *personal love* rather than Divine Love. He did not realize that the distressed energy from the people being helped had infiltrated his body. This led to a general malaise that resulted in his untimely death. Divine Love, not personal love, should have been used.

All About Divine Love

Today, the energy of Divine Love is very strong in the universe. *It is evident to those of us who work with Divine Love every day that it is the only energy that should be used for effective healing.* This is why you need to learn about and utilize Divine Love in your self-healing and in helping others.

The second case involved a woman who evidenced love for God and other people, but not for herself. As a result of having engaged in some socially unacceptable behaviors, she could not love herself. She tried to use the At Oneness Healing System to release the root cause of cancer plaguing her body, but it was an incomplete release because she would not love and forgive herself for her own past transgressions. The cancer accelerated and she died within weeks. ***The lesson here is that we are each held accountable by the Creator to love the Creator, to love other people, and to love ourselves. Otherwise, Divine Love may not correct our problems. Divine Love is a powerful gift, but we must be willing to change our limited beliefs to properly utilize it.***

The third case involved someone I had known for many years. This person had been on several webinars and had used the Petitions we teach to correct many life traumas. Things had been going fairly well until one day when I got a phone call asking for help to release excruciating pain. We did the Petitions, but I noticed that nothing was happening. I told my friend to go to a medical doctor immediately for help. My friend called me days later to report that inoperable cancer had been found in several organs.

I asked my friend to concentrate with internal Spirit and Divine Love on why the problem was there. My friend knew immediately something was wrong, and between gut wrenching sobs, told me the reason: My friend did not consider "self" worthy enough to ask the Creator for help *until it was too late*. My friend finally understood the need to release any sense of unworthiness and then *ask* the Creator directly for help through Petitions.

Sadly, my friend died shortly after our last talk, but did understand that there had been a *choice not made* (to release unworthiness). If you consider yourself "unworthy," you must release this limitation if you really want healing help. Then you can *ask* the Creator for help directly and you will usually get relief with your Petitions.

What You Can Heal

You can heal just about anything if you stick with the At Oneness Healing System.

All About Divine Love

You will need to:

Always stay connected to Divine Love. (You will learn how to do this in a later chapter.)

Continue with your At Oneness Healing System long enough to heal yourself at the deepest level.

Stick with *one* symptom throughout the healing effort. Do not change to a new symptom until the old symptom is fully corrected. If in doubt, ask the Creator for guidance.

Chapter 6

Understand the

At Oneness Healing System (AOHS)

There are several terms used in this book that will be explained as we encounter them.

In our 2015 webinars, we gave our attendees a "Protocol" to follow. A Protocol is a time-based set of instructions. The Protocol eliminates one of the key problems that some people have, which is the tendency to disconnect from Divine Love before a healing is complete.

There are many subtle components to under-stand while working with Divine Love in the At Oneness Healing System (AOHS). The two Petitions we use are the "At Oneness Petition" and the "Lovingness Petition." These two Petitions produce a very powerful inter-action with the Divine that are used in a disciplined manner with the Protocol.

Understand the AOHS

I am always asked to explain the difference between conventional prayer and At Oneness Healing System Petitions. There are significant differences between prayer and Petitions:

> The first difference between Petitions and prayer is that Petitions require *you* to do something rather than expecting the Creator to do all the work in answering your request. To use Petitions effectively requires that you understand you are using a *spiritual* healing process rather than a *mental* process.

> The second difference is that you are interacting *actively* with the Divine and *participating in your spiritual, mental, and physical healing while Divine Love works with your Spirit to accomplish healing*.

> The third difference is that *two Petitions are used as a pair in a timed sequence (called a Protocol) until the condition is corrected.*

In this chapter, we are going to look at the key things you need to do to be effective in Divine Love healing. We will study this in sections so that you become aware of the changes that you need to make in your life to achieve a

Divine Love Self Healing

permanent healing.

For example, if you use the Petitions to release yourself from an addiction, that addiction is removed from your body. If you continue to surround yourself with others who have the addiction you've released, your life in that environment can be difficult, with too many temptations.

However, when you begin living a life based upon Divine Love, you can live successfully in *any* environment without reacquiring your prior addiction. This is true for drug, food, sex, alcohol, and most other addictions.

Fast versus Slow Healing

As I mentioned earlier, when people have fear, doubt, or uncertainty, it may take longer to clear out those conditions before true healing can begin. In addition, people experiencing slow healing may have other conditions that need to be cleared, such as:

Mental blocks to accepting spiritual truth. This occurs in individuals who are fearful or reluctant to examine the truth about themselves.

The inability to discriminate between spiritual truths and any spiritual untruths because of misunderstandings that have accumulated over the years. People who accept what they are told without confirming the truth can become confused when presented with ideas which do not fit in with their concept of spirituality. Others have problems defining what a spiritual life is. These folks typically seek a spiritual identity outside themselves; they may view Divinity as something to which one can only aspire, not achieve.

We do not teach religion. What we *do* teach is that you can have a direct spiritual connection to the Divine by utilizing your Spirit. This connection is like a secure satellite telephone link to the Creator. That link enables you to Petition and converse with the Creator to receive guidance.

Frustration over individual healing rates. This usually occurs with someone who keeps disconnecting from Divine Love while his system is trying to heal. Remember: *Always stay connected to Divine Love.* How to stay connected is presented in Chapter 7.

When people have long-term chronic disorders, they often manifest thoughts

Divine Love Self Healing

of hopelessness. We see cases where people cannot attain wellness until they are willing to allow themselves to *experience* and *accept* healing. Of course, part of the hopelessness is a bad manifestation, but there is another component:. It is the false idea that a person is stuck with a health problem because their ancestors had a similar problem. We know today that people can release these false underlying ideas because DNA can be changed through Divine Love healing.

Everything that people buy generally comes with operating instructions. When people use the At Oneness Healing System and do not get immediate results, often their response is to assume that they have done something wrong. However, if you follow the time-proven methods that have been developed, you cannot do the At Oneness Healing System incorrectly.

Sometimes people get distracted and do not do the Petitions as given, or they disconnect themselves from Divine Love and do not reconnect. Remember that when you disconnect from Divine Love, healing stops; when you reconnect yourself to Divine Love, healing resumes.

Understand the AOHS

The good news is that when people correctly use the At Oneness Healing System, all of the above conditions can be cleared and true permanent healing can take place.

Review of Basic Spiritual Truths

Let's establish a factual spiritual baseline so that you can better understand what is happening in our healing system.

We are all spiritual beings with human bodies; we are not bodies seeking a spirit.

Each of us has an internal Spirit, a Soul, and a Mind in the form of what are called energy bodies. These are layered throughout our system and in space around the body. We are each like an energy hologram, and holograms can be changed.

Your Soul is influenced by your current and past lives and carries energy imprints that can adversely affect your *layers, your energy bodies.*

Your Mind contains a complete record of your experiences in this life and your mind influences your decision-making abilities. Your mind can also *resist* healing your energy layers.

Divine Love Self Healing

Divine Love is the Creator's Love and it is the most powerful energy force in the universe. Divine Love is in and around you and exists throughout the universe. It is a *neutral* energy until it is activated by your Spirit to do something (as in your Petitions).

We can all use our Spiritual intention to send and receive Divine Love instantaneously anywhere in the world, to affect persons, places, or things.

To avoid emotional attachments, it is very important to utilize Divine Love and not personal love.

We utilize our internal Spirit because it allows us to operate at the highest energy level our bodies can accommodate and produces far better results than any other transmission method.

Only your Spirit controls your healing rate; no one else is involved. This is important to understand because your Spirit regulates how fast your system is healing layer by layer. Sometimes your Spirit is healing something in you that is more important than what you specified in your symptom.

On a given *layer,* once the primary healing is done, you may not feel anything happening.

Understand the AOHS

You might then falsely assume that healing is not working or that you are finished. What is really happening is that your Spirit is healing individual cells after the energy that made you unwell has been cleared from your system.

As you digest these spiritual truths, you begin to fully appreciate spiritual healing as we teach it.

Surrendering to the Creator

One of the Petitions uses the word "surrender," which causes some people to become defensive; they don't want to lose personal control of their lives. It is very difficult for them to surrender to an unseen force called the Creator. This occurs because of their interpretation of the word.

What I mean by surrender is that I recognize that many of life's problems cannot be solved by any actions that we personally can take or have already taken. *A spiritual intercession is necessary.* We are asking the Divine to orchestrate our healing.

To me, surrendering is also my willingness to accept the Creator's guidance, so that the best choices are made to solve problems that appear in my life.

Divine Love Self Healing

Surrendering does not mean that you should do anything that you know would be harmful. The Creator will not mislead you or manipulate you. I think of surrender more in terms of opening up a conversation with the Creator, similar to getting together for coffee or tea with a close friend. You can discuss your life problems with the Creator and receive in return guidance to help give meaning and purpose to your life.

Science Behind Petitions

When I worked in a private lab with Dr. Marcel Vogel, an eminent IBM scientist, we developed crystal devices that amplified our energy fields. These devices enabled us to help people release their energy problems.

Over time we found that our individual energy levels increased and we were able to achieve the same results without using a device of any kind. Now you can also achieve results, without crystals or any other device, because Divine Love has increased in frequency over the last several years. This frequency has been measured by proprietary equipment.

This increase in energy provides everyone the same access to Divine Love at whatever energy level is required for healing, without the need for large group support as was taught years ago. Hence, the At Oneness Healing System can become the norm for spiritual healing.

As your healing progresses, you clear out the harmful energy layers in your body. As you clear the energy layers with the two Petitions, you achieve the alignment condition I call "being at one with the Divine." As your body aligns, healing is greatly simplified.

Research from around the world has shown that hostile words negatively affect our DNA and cellular structure. I learned this in early 1980 while working with Dr. Vogel. It is important to realize that genetic DNA problems can be changed with Divine Love.

Background and Healing Reports

We receive many e-mails from people expressing self-doubt about their abilities to be healed. Some people are just skeptical, which is fine; I too am a very strong skeptic. Others with low self esteem feel that they are not worthy, but know this: We are all equally worthy of being healed.

For a better understanding of the healing programs and the differences between personal love and Divine Love, I suggest you watch the "Background" video found under the

Divine Love Self Healing

"Webinar" tab on our website:

http://www.worldserviceinstitute.org

You should also read the Healing Reports written by people from around the world who have applied the principles we teach to heal depression, heart disease, addictions, and a variety of cancers. Their successes should inspire you. Notice that many of the Reports reference contact with the Creator or Angels. As you continue working with the At Oneness Healing system, you can establish your personal connection to the Creator and receive detailed guidance on just exactly how to proceed.

Angels and Beliefs

I am always amazed at how people answer my questions about angels. Most people believe that angels exist, but are surprised to learn that we can communicate and even have full conversations with angels. It is perfectly fine to have a healthy skepticism about angels and their existence, but please be open to exploring spiritual truths. Here's one spiritual truth:

Two or more angels are assigned to help you in your life.

Just start a conversation with the Creator and

your angels. Once they deem that you are ready, they will respond to you. The feedback concerning your life problems will be an eye-opening experience.

Healing Others

Parents frequently ask if they can use Petitions to change the behavior of their teenage or adult children. Please understand that you cannot manipulate a solution with Divine Love, even when you believe something "better" is possible. Each person must decide for himself whether he will work with Divine Love healing.

Trying to correct significant mental conditions in others is also not advised. People with psychotic disorders can best be helped by trained professionals using the AOHS; that in-struction is beyond the scope of this book.

Our beloved pets and other creatures do not need the At Oneness Petition. When the animal is present with you, you can use the Lovingness Petition while placing your hands on the animal; this physical contact is optional.

When the animal is not with you, just use the Lovingness Petition.

Divine Love Self Healing

Human Energy Layers

In Divine Love spiritual healing, it does not matter how an illness is contracted or where it is located in the physical body. Removing the harmful energy that causes illness *is* important, however. That energy can exist in multiple layers and at various locations in the body. The harmful energy is intertwined with the energies of Soul, Mind, and the physical body.

Harmful energy attracts additional harmful energy. When the harmful energy builds up to a high enough level, it is difficult to remove through healing modalities that do not use Divine Love.

Our bodies have hundreds of energy layers, both inside and outside the body. The first layer in a healthy person is located outside the body about 4 inches from the skin's surface. Ordinarily, the body heals energetically from the outside to the inside of a person's core being. Each energy layer is capable of interacting with thoughts and actions.

The layers expand and contract as a function of breathing and wellness.

When a person breathes in, he compresses his layers toward his core; when he breathes out, his layers expand to their normal position.

Understand the AOHS

A person experiencing mental or emotional trauma may project energy layers several feet from the body. Or, energy layers may collapse on one side of the body, frequently causing severe pain.

When energy layers are allowed to expand in an uncontrolled fashion, we begin to absorb emotional energy from other people that can adversely impact our own energy layers. Over time, when someone has severe emotional problems, the layers can become very dense "clumps" of emotional energy that can also prevent proper functioning.

Alignment with the Creator

Years ago we noticed that when people were living life with a loving outlook, they were able to heal much faster than people exhibiting a negative or unloving attitude. People who are living *unloving* lives are by definition not in alignment with the Divine Love of the Creator.

The At Oneness Petition clears the spiritual, mental, and physical energies that prevent us from being completely aligned with the Creator and then Divine Love *correctly aligns* our bodies energetically. Once aligned, healing of Soul, Mind, and Body becomes simple, rapid, and complete.

Divine Love Self Healing

The Lovingness Petition uses a *symptom* to address a condition. Illness can originate from two distinct conditions operating separately or together:

1. Emotional energies stored in the body.

2. Trauma-related energies caused by accidents or radiation, or by toxins in our food, drink, or air.

The healing approach used for these two distinct problem sources is very important. We found that about half of all illness manifests from stored emotional energy. If these emotions are not released, over time they will literally "plug" your energy layers.

When energy layers become plugged, cells lose their ability to communicate with each other. The cells may die, they may begin to mutate, or they may interrupt body functions. This process eventually produces a variety of symptoms that can become life-threatening diseases.

People may or may not be aware of their energy blockages. Blockages caused by post traumatic stress may be complex; other ill-nesses are more easily recognized when they originate from a purely *physical* cause. An underlying *cause* can be introduced at any time in a person's life, even genetically introduced at conception.

At one time I taught students to use a Lovingness Petition to correct *emotions* first. If various ailments like pain, addictions, dys-functional behavior, and other life-threatening diseases had an underlying *emotional cause*, then those ailments often disappeared once the emotional energy was released. However, in cases of long-standing problems, this ap-proach could take several days. Then if a person still had a physical symptom, we would go through the Petition pair again until the symptom was gone. In complex cases this two-step approach worked, but took too long because the Petitions were taking out *all* emo-tional energies, even those unrelated to the client's symptom.

Today we use *one* Lovingness Petition to correct both a physical symptom *and* the associated emotional energies all at once. This usually facilitates a complete healing in less elapsed time.

If the problem is not corrected by day five, we do a past life regression to identify what is interfering, then remove the Soul debt using the Lovingness Petition, and finally, begin the two-Petition Protocol again.

Divine Love Self Healing

Interestingly, all Divine Love healing works the same way! Any energy associated with un-loving thoughts, words, or deeds, collects in our human energy layers. Bad energy from trauma-related conditions also collects in our energy layers. When Petitions are used cor-rectly, the energy making a person ill is broken up and is purged from the body.

Activating Divine Love

Divine Love, the universal energy from the Creator, exists everywhere in a neutral state. When you initiate a Petition, your Spirit acti-vates the energy of Divine Love and then your Spirit utilizes Divine Love to effect a change in your body. Your Spirit works with Divine Love unless you disconnect from Divine Love before your healing is complete. Should this occur, Divine Love returns to a neutral state and nothing more happens until *you* reconnect your system to Divine Love. Now you understand the importance of always staying connected.

Harmful energy can exist in some or all of your energy layers. When dealing with a systemic blood disease or sepsis, for example, it is likely that all layers have been contaminated by the harmful energy causing the illness.

For those of you exhibiting major inflammation

in your body, you should note that there is a spiritual basis for this. Your spirit and mind interact and cause energetic and physical friction, resulting in inflammation or swelling that does not go away. People with weight control problems will see improvement when they use Petitions correctly to eliminate the inflammation in their bodies.

Symptom Return

Occasionally, people report that their symptoms return after a few days. This usually occurs either because they stopped the petitions before healing was complete or they disconnected from Divine Love. This problem is usually corrected by using the *Simplified Protocol* described in Chapter 7.

About Other Healing Modalities

People frequently want to continue with other healing modalities while their systems are going through the At Oneness Healing System spiritual healing process. We know that many practitioners provide services that are very helpful, but there is a note of caution for someone going through a healing.

We suggest that you verify that a practitioner is working with Divine Love during your healing

Divine Love Self Healing

time. The reason for this is that if a practitioner is energetically stressed or upset, he can transfer that distressed energy into your body while you are healing.

One individual mentioned that his practitioner was a longtime friend. When I asked whether the practitioner always utilized Divine Love, the individual did not know.

Since you usually would *not* know whether your practitioner was using Divine Love, the best practice might be for you to avoid other modalities until your body heals.

Obviously, if you are under the care of a medical doctor you should continue with his treatment program. As your spiritual healing progresses, your symptoms should clear and you can ask your physician to retest you, or reduce and eventually eliminate any medications that the doctor no longer feels you need, based upon your test results.

Chapter 7

At Oneness Healing System
(AOHS)

Staying Connected to Divine Love

Let us first understand what is meant by *accelerated healing*. There are three fairly obvious factors to consider:

1. When you have multiple illnesses, it should be obvious that it will take longer for you to heal than if you had just one straightforward problem. If you are very ill, it may take your body significant time to process the energy of Divine Love in your body.

2. A person comfortable with our spiritual healing process and who has a single symptom frequently experiences instantaneous healing during a webinar. Others may take anywhere from hours to days to achieve the same level of healing,

Divine Love Self Healing

so please don't compare your progress to others. You are a unique individual and your Spirit knows exactly what needs to be done.

3. If you are distracted or become unloving towards yourself or others, you may unknowingly disconnect yourself from Divine Love, and then all healing ceases. Healing does not resume until you re-initiate a Divine Love connection.

Reconnecting to Divine Love is as simple as saying, "With my Spirit, I accept Divine Love throughout my entire system," then pulsing your breath to reset your Divine Love connection. Many people copy this phrase, then post it as a reminder on a bathroom mirror or a kitchen cupboard. If you repeat this state-ment every time you see it, it will help you stay connected to Divine Love and experience faster healing.

By always staying connected to Divine Love, you will transition your entire system into a spiritual mode where you will be living a life of Divine Love. What does it mean to live life this way? Very simply, even when chaos erupts around you, you will be able to function without being driven by your emotions. And, you will be able to function with clarity while others may become upset and lose their objectivity.

At Oneness Healing System

Also, each time you audibly state your intent to reconnect to Divine Love, you enable Divine Love to bypass any resistance to change that may come from your subconscious mind. This is vitally important to facilitate healing.

Remember that if you perceive that a physical symptom has left or is diminished, but it suddenly returns, it is quite likely that you have disconnected from Divine Love.

Feeling Divine Love

If you are experiencing energy healing for the first time, you may not know the many ways Divine Love energy *feels* in your body. You might feel heat, a tingle, a vibration, a cooling effect, or even see swirling energy around your body; it is all normal.

Since everyone has angelic support, some people find it more assuring to ask their Angels to assist them in processing Divine Love. Years ago on our webinars, we always invited the Angels to participate. Now, with the energy of Divine Love so high, Angelic participation is optional. Choose to work whichever way brings you the most comfort.

The simple act of accepting Divine Love fills your body with the right amount of Divine Love

Divine Love Self Healing

energy to heal your system. There is always enough Divine Love for the most complex healing, so you no longer need group support. You are self-healing in conjunction with the Creator's Divine Love.

Petition Overview

For many years, Petitions were developed to address specific conditions. Eventually we were able to distill all of these Petitions into just two powerful Petitions for the At Oneness Healing System.

The first Petition is the "At Oneness Petition." If you have the luxury of time, this single Petition could take care of your health problems.

However, since most people want faster results, a second Petition, the "Lovingness Petition," allows the user to specify one symptom to be healed.

The actual wording of the Petitions comes later. The key thing to know is that the Petitions are used as a pair for our *Simplified Protocol*.

You could say your two Petitions just once a day, *provided that you stay connected to Divine Love*. You can also do more Petition

At Oneness Healing System

pairs each day, although that does not automatically increase your healing rate. Saying any Petition that contains the words *Spirit* and *Divine Love* will reconnect you to Divine Love. Remember that your Spirit controls healing.

Fill your time with your normal daily activities. You do *not* have to meditate, be isolated, or shield yourself from the public while you use the At Oneness Healing System.

However, to facilitate your healing, it is crucial for you to stay connected to Divine Love as much as possible. Learning to "stay connected" as a daily habit will not only speed recovery, but also prevent you from acquiring and holding harmful energy.

Recall that when your Spirit activates Divine Love in your Petition, Divine Love *shatters, layer by layer,* the bad energy that is interfering with you. The shattered energy fragments are removed energetically with more Divine Love as you breathe in and out.

Since bad energy can permeate many layers in our internal energy fields, it follows that the bad energy comes out layer by layer. To assure that the bad energy is totally removed, we suggest continuing the Protocol for three additional days after a symptom has disappeared.

Divine Love Self Healing

For complete healing to occur, Divine Love *must* be present in its activated state throughout your process. *It is imperative that you stay connected to Divine Love or your healing stops.* If you are not proceeding satisfactorily in your healing, it is usually because you unknowingly disconnected from Divine Love.

The At Oneness Healing System Petitions

Later I will show you how to use the Petitions with the Protocol to get results. Right now I want to give you the Petitions and describe how best to say them.

The At Oneness Petition

Say the At Oneness Petition aloud:

"With my Spirit, I accept Divine Love throughout my entire system. I surrender my entire being to the Creator."

"I ask my spirit to identify every situation and every cause that separates me from the Creator. I release to the Creator all of those situations and causes. I ask that the Creator heal my system according to Divine will."

Now inhale, close your mouth, and *pulse* out breath lightly through the nose *once*, as if blowing your nose.

The Lovingness Petition

This Petition is used for simultaneous *physical* and *emotional* healing. It requires that you pay particular attention to staying connected to Divine Love.

Say the Lovingness Petition for physical and emotional healing aloud:

"With my Spirit and Divine Love, I accept Divine Love throughout my entire system. I focus on all the causes of my (*name one symptom*) and all the causes of unlovingness towards myself, creation and the Creator and release all of the causes to the Creator and ask that the condition be healed according to Divine will."

Now inhale, close your mouth, and pulse out breath lightly through the nose once, as if blowing your nose.

Simplified Protocol

It is simple for you to do a healing on yourself and stay connected to Divine Love by using the

Divine Love Self Healing

following protocol with the Petition pair. Do the Petitions exactly as described in the protocol below, then stay connected to Divine Love so that the two Petitions can work through your system.

1. Say the **At Oneness Petition** aloud *just once* and then pulse breath one time.

2. Wait 5 minutes.

3. Say the **Lovingness Petition** aloud *just once* and then pulse breath one time.

4. Wait 5 minutes.

5. **Stay connected to Divine Love**. About every 15 minutes, say aloud, "I accept Divine Love throughout my entire system" and pulse your breath. (You may want to use a timer or your cell phone alarm to alert you when it is time to do Step 5.

6. Repeat step 5 until the symptom is cleared. Then continue step 5 for three additional days to make sure that you have cleared all the energy layers.

This Simplified Protocol is easy to use, but you must stay connected to Divine Love as best you can for it to work effectively. Remember that when you are upset by anything, you can *unknowingly* disconnect yourself from Divine Love and healing stops. Healing does not resume until you reconnect with Divine Love. Resume the two Petitions until the problem is corrected.

After 5 days, if your problem still remains, do a past life regression on yourself (if this is acceptable to you). Release the "Soul debt" using the Lovingness Petition and then repeat your original Protocol from Step 1.

Duration of Protocol Use

The Protocol should be continued in adults for at least three days following the disappearance of the symptom. This helps to assure that the energetic root cause of the problem is completely removed. Step 5 is not used with children below the age of five.

When you are correcting something that you can see or feel, the healing may be obvious. However, if you have had a major disease, you should go to your physician to obtain whatever testing is needed to prove that the symptom is healed. Ten days of Protocol use can usually correct most problems, provided that you stay connected to Divine Love using the Simplified Protocol.

Divine Love Self Healing

We strongly believe that there should be a strong bond between the patient, the physician, and the spiritual healing process. However, it is the responsibility of the patient to correctly implement the healing system. We do not accept any liability for use or misuse. Your wellness and recovery are between you and the Creator.

Recap

Your healing process will stop if either of the two following conditions exist:

1. You do not stay connected to Divine Love.

There is no excuse for not staying connected to Divine Love. If you make an excuse, it demonstrates that you do not care enough about yourself to follow through.

Staying connected to Divine Love is necessary for the best results. Staying connected has been discussed multiple times because it is one of the keys to wellness. Avoid it or skip it, and you may not get the results you seek in a reasonable time.

2. You do not accept the healing.

At Oneness Healing System

The principal reason that people don't accept healing is *fear* of something. As you continue to use the At Oneness Petition, your fears will gradually clear. You cannot rush this process because your Spirit and Divine Love are in charge.

If you are not using *both* Petitions or are using them incorrectly, the healing system works, but your progress is lessened; your Spirit stops the process so that you cannot hurt yourself! In the following chapters you will see how all this works together.

If there is a spiritual problem from your past, it can be a key impediment to your healing progress. If you use the Simplified Protocol for 5 days but do not observe any improvement, it is likely that there is a spiritual problem that needs to be cleared out.

The fastest way to improve your situation is to study the chapter on past life regression. It is sufficiently simple that you can do it yourself. If you do not *believe* in past lives, then just keep repeating the Petition pair and periodically check to see if you have a connection to the Creator. When you have that connection, ask the Creator how to proceed.

A significant impediment to your progress can be caused by your environment or your attitude. If you are in a hostile environment, are constantly upset, or if you consistently respond negatively to people and situations in your life, it is likely that after doing a Petition you will immediately disconnect yourself from Divine Love! However, if you concentrate on staying connected to Divine Love, over time you should see a dramatic improvement.

These various conditions have been brought to your attention because the results you seek may take time, but we know the process works; do not give up! If you need help understanding and getting results, register for one of our At Oneness Healing System Webinars, available periodically throughout the year.

Buts

Frequently I hear, "If I am in pain, are you telling me that I have to sit around for *5 days* before I *might* get relief? And even then I might have to do a past life regression and start over?"

Not quite. Here is some good news: When you use the At Oneness Healing System and Simplified Protocol, both the *emotional* and *physical* causes of your *symptom* are captured! The healing is very powerful and operates more quickly; *but* you cannot skip steps in the Simplified Protocol! If you do not get the desired results, you always can do a past life regression, *but,* if this is not part of your belief system, ask the Creator what to do. *But,* if you do not yet have a connection to the Creator that you trust, do the Simplified Protocol until you can make the connection.

Pop-Up Symptoms

As your body clears, you might experience an unexpected secondary symptom different from the one you were using. This could be an ache or pain, or an emotion that you did not have when you started your Petitions. Simply put that secondary symptom into a Lovingness Petition and say that single Petition aloud every 5 minutes until the pop-up symptom is completely gone.

Then, go back to Step 1 of the Protocol to start over. Deal with pop-ups as they come up; otherwise, maintain your Protocol. It is that simple; do not make it more complicated.

Correct Subconscious Resistance to Healing

Subconscious resistance to healing is a common problem that can be quickly over-come, once you understand the principle. I have heard it said that people limit themselves in various ways no matter what they are doing and that this is a normal human response.

Divine Love Self Healing

I disagree with that opinion!

People often try to justify perceived failures. Below are some examples of remarks driven by the subconscious:

"I have (*fill in the blank*) and can't possibly get well."

"I can't find the job I want."

"Other people are getting well, but I am not, so the Creator must have abandoned me, or is punishing me."

"I didn't heal rapidly, so this healing system doesn't work for me."

"I must be doing something wrong."

The problem with the above statements in most cases is that they represent *false subconscious* beliefs that adversely influence the ability to heal. To understand how to become free of this thinking, you need to better understand the power of *intention* and then eliminate any hidden subconscious belief that is holding you back.

Intention is thought energy that can be moved through space. When you repeatedly tell yourself that you cannot heal, you can build a resistive wall of energy both in and around yourself. This wall becomes so powerful that you become trapped in your belief, unable to escape your thought. In effect, you got what you asked for!

Over time, the At Oneness Petition will clear subconscious resistance, but all Petitions are subject to your Free Will, from either your active mind or your subconscious mind.

The good news: If you use the At Oneness Healing System and find yourself plodding along, only getting partial results, use the Lovingness Petition and a symptom of "all my subconscious hidden resistance" as you use the Protocol. Do this for several days to quickly and completely clear out false subconscious beliefs.

Helping Young Children

When you are dealing with young children, use the At Oneness Healing System just as you would use it for yourself. For very young children and babies, you can hold the child in your arms or on your lap.

Don't expect children to use the Simplified Protocol; use the two Petitions as discussed. If the child can read, let him read and use the Petitions, but pay attention to the timing. By

Divine Love Self Healing

this I mean that you should allow time to adjust and benefit from each Petition rather than rushing to the next step.

Say the At Oneness Petition and then wait about one-half hour for it to complete. Then use the Lovingness Petition and wait for two hours.

In the interim between Petitions, children can play or otherwise entertain themselves. We suggest that they not play with electronic games, computers, or watch television, as those actions distract the child.

We suggest that the two Petitions be used as a *pair* at least three times a day until the symptom has cleared. Then do both Petition pairs three times a day for an additional three days. The purpose of this is to make make sure that the symptom has been completely cleared out of the child.

Chapter 8

Deeper Understandings

As our webinar attendees gain experience, they often ask more in-depth questions that cannot easily be answered during a webinar; we have therefore added question-and-answer webinars periodically throughout the year. Since some of you did not have the benefit of those webinars, I will present the material in this chapter.

The Role of Focus in Petitions

A few people reported that they did not get any results. In questioning them, I learned that they had exhibited one or more of the following behaviors:

1. They read the Petitions as if they were a newspaper article, then dashed off to execute the next task on their daily "to do" list, without correctly completing the Petitions.

Divine Love Self Healing

2.   They skipped Petitions or did them infrequently because they were "too busy," or "just forgot."

3.   They were distracted by their own mind chatter or various interruptions.

All three of the above behaviors represents a loss of needed *focus*. To understand focus, try the following exercise: Pinch the skin at the tip of the first finger on your left hand (using the first finger and thumb fingernails of your right hand) until you feel a slight pain in your fingertip. Then gradually increase the pinch until it hurts more. Notice that as you pinch harder, your attention is drawn to the point of pain; you recognize how much your finger hurts. That is an example of *focus*.

In healing, *focus* is:

Concentrating on stating the correct Petition without distractions.

Concentrating on staying on the Protocol schedule. If necessary, make a written schedule and log your planned activity. A timer is also useful.

Concentrating spiritually on accepting Divine Love (activating Divine Love) for a few minutes, without interruptions.

Deeper Understandings

Become "At One with the Divine"

As you become more aware of your behavior, you can take immediate steps to release whatever thoughts. actions, or beliefs no longer serve you. By releasing them, you deepen your connection to the Divine. You may wake one morning with a more positive and blissful outlook. Thus, you can change behavior and rise above any chaos.

Here's an example: Suppose that your elbow hurts. You use the two petitions as explained in this book, and soon the pain is gone. Perhaps you get "insight" into a cause of the problem, e.g., an *unloving* action such as swearing at people when you are upset.

A week later you find yourself exhibiting a different unloving act, perhaps making a dis-paraging remark about someone, and you notice that your elbow is once again becoming tender. Now, use the two petitions to perma-nently release the effect of "all disparaging remarks."

Your elbow is giving you feedback about yourself by drawing your attention to how you behave! As you continue to recognize the root causes for your symptoms and release all of those causes, you progress toward living your

Divine Love Self Healing

life in harmony with the Divine.

Coping with the Environment

People often ask me how they can cope with environmental contamination when they do not have access to, or cannot afford, food and drink that they know is absolutely safe to consume. Drinking water can be contaminated by chemicals and medicines getting into water supplies; the problem seems to be getting worse.

What can you do to help protect yourself and your family from ingesting harmful materials?

One easy-to-use method is to focus on your food or drink with your internal spirit and Divine Love, plus the *intention to clear* the material so that it is safe to consume. Then pulse your breath. I do this whenever I eat, whether at home or away.

You may have read scientific reports about the increase in cosmic radiation coming from deep space or from radiation elsewhere on earth. I made reference in <u>Being at One with the Divine</u> to the people in the area of Fukushima, Japan, after the nuclear reactor disasters in 2011.

Deeper Understandings

In a special Mass Consciousness Webinar, we assembled a large group together, doing a healing to protect all living things exposed to the radiation.

As of July 2015, according to a NOVA TV special on that disaster, no one has died from radiation poisoning! International scientists (not on NOVA) have found that, although some of the people at the plant were exposed sufficiently to have warranted significant radiation sickness by now, it has not happened.

If you are concerned about cosmic or nuclear radiation poisoning from space, the ground, or the atmosphere, gather a group of people together and apply the Mass Consciousness Petitions as described in our Mass Con-sciousness webinar (videos available on our website). Those videos will show you exactly how to proceed.

Breathing

Most people who use our petitions use them correctly, but some do not take advantage of two important breathing techniques: the Breath Pulse and 4-Cycle Breathing.

Let's look at the purpose of these two breathing techniques. After stating a Petition aloud we suggest people draw in a breath, close their

Divine Love Self Healing

mouth, then pulse the breath out through the nose, fairly hard, as if you were blowing your nose. This causes an At Oneness Healing System Petition to move to persons, places or things.

The Breath Pulse releases the Petition into the space surrounding your body, so that the Petition can work upon your energy fields from the outside to the deepest part of you. We find that this speeds up personal healing.

If you do not use a Breath Pulse because of pulmonary limitations, the Petitions still work, but will act more slowly.

After the Petition is spoken aloud and *after* the Breath Pulse, you can speed up your healing by doing 4-Cycle Breathing as described here:

Cycle 1-Breathe in deeply and very slowly until your lungs are full.

Cycle 2-Hold your breath for a slow count of five or more.

Cycle 3-Breathe out very slowly and completely, emptying your lungs.

Cycle 4-Do not breathe in again for a slow count of five or more.

Deeper Understandings

Repeat 4-Cycle Breathing as frequently as you like whenever it suits you!

Thousands of people use 4-Cycle Breathing to effectively speed healing. By oxygenating the body it helps clear the detrimental energies that Divine Love dissolves in your body. Just do this technique for five minutes anytime, and notice a remarkable improvement in how you feel!

For disease correction, do 4-Cycle Breathing more often and for a longer time interval.

Chapter 9

Healing a Single Symptom

We will study two actual composite cases. *Composite* means that people can have a mixture of ailments. It does not matter what the illnesses are because with the Divine Love At Oneness Healing System, healing proceeds in exactly the same manner in all cases. That is why the next two chapters are crucial to your understanding.

Both cases illustrate how *harmful energy* is removed from body energy layers using the At Oneness Healing System. For teaching simplicity, we define the harmful energy as being confined to a limited number of layers so that we can discuss each case without becoming overwhelmed with detail. In most people, harmful energy actually penetrates into many more layers.

Healing a Single Symptom

Harry's case is given in this chapter. Sally's case is in the next chapter.

The Lovingness Petition was improved in March 2016 to remove both *physical* and *emotional* causes at one time, provided that the Simplified Protocol is followed. However, at the time of Harry's healing, this was not available; he used the Lovingness Petition that appeared in <u>Being at One with the Divine</u> and "I accept Divine Love" to stay connected to Divine Love as his body healed. You will see the current Lovingness Petition applied in Sally's case.

July 2015: Harry is a 60-year-old active man; he runs a technical consulting business from his home. He developed a malignant tumor on his brain stem. The tumor was diagnosed and validated through extensive tests using modern diagnostic medical equipment.

His tumor penetrated through many *layers* of Harry's body. Harry decided to use the At Oneness Healing System using the two Petition pair, repeating the pair three times a day, as was taught in 2015.

As Harry used the At Oneness Petition, the spiritual, mental, and physical energies interfering with Harry's alignment with the Creator began to clear. When this happened, Harry's energy layers became *aligned* with the Creator. (This does not mean that Harry *became* the Creator; it simply means that his energy was aligned for rapid healing.) The Lovingness Petition could then be used effectively.

Harry's First Pair Usage

To begin, Harry said aloud the At Oneness Petition and pulsed his breath once. Then, in the hour that followed, he stayed connected to Divine Love by repeatedly saying "I accept Divine Love," followed by a pulsed breath. He did this about every 10 minutes.

Harry's Spirit began to direct his alignment. During the first hour, Harry's Spirit cleared his body through five layers as quickly as possible while stabilizing him and preventing any discomfort.

At the beginning of the second hour, Harry said the Lovingness Petition as follows: "I release my *tumor* to the Creator and ask that the condition be healed." Then he pulsed breath once.

Upon saying the Lovingness Petition aloud, Harry's Spirit began to clear out the bad energy causing the tumor throughout the five layers.

Healing a Single Symptom

Harry's Spirit could not complete more layers because Harry had not yet completely *aligned* beyond his fifth layer. *The At Oneness Petition must complete a given layer before the Lovingness Petition can complete its clearing function on that same layer.*

Once again, Harry's Spirit maintained balance throughout Harry's body as Harry said, "I accept Divine Love," followed by a breath pulse every 15 minutes. This kept Harry connected to Divine Love for the next two hours as his layers continued to heal.

Total elapsed time: 3 hours.

At this point, Harry could have taken a break to do some work in his consulting business. If he decided to work for several hours, he could say, "I accept Divine Love" at 10 or 15 minute intervals to be sure that he stayed connected to Divine Love.

However, because he was totally dedicated to becoming well, Harry wanted to start his second round of Petitions right away.

Harry's Second Pair Usage

Harry said the At Oneness Petition. During the next hour, every ten minutes he said, "I accept Divine Love" and pulsed his breath just once each time. During that hour, his Spirit continued to clear more layers.

After an hour, Harry again said aloud the Lovingness Petition, exactly as he did before, keeping himself connected to Divine Love. In the next two hours his Spirit was able to complete healing on more layers.

At this point Harry had accomplished a complete healing on several layers, but he was not yet finished.

Total elapsed time: 6 hours.

Harry could do whatever he wanted to during the day as long as he stayed connected to Divine Love. This is especially important to anyone who wants or needs to remain active.
Harry continued by starting the petition pair a third time.

Harry's Third Pair Usage

Harry said the At Oneness Petition and stayed connected to Divine Love as another hour progressed. Spirit aligned Harry with the Creator through even more layers.

In the next hour, Harry said the Lovingness Petition as was given above. Harry's Spirit worked on clearing more harmful energy from

Healing a Single Symptom

Harry's body. Because the bulk of the harmful energy was in early layers, and those layers were now clear, Harry's Spirit easily cleared more layers during the next two hours. Of course Harry stayed connected to Divine Love during this period.

Harry's Further Pair Usage

Harry continued to work with the Petition pair for several more days and his Spirit cleared him through all his layers for both At Oneness and Lovingness Petitions.

On Day 4, Harry asked the Creator if his healing was complete. Harry received a positive confirmation. He then scheduled a follow-up appointment with his doctor for a complete lab/exam to medically determine the status of his health.

Harry was not surprised when he was told that there was no remaining evidence of any tumor. Harry knew he was healed. If Harry had *not* gotten a clean bill of health at this point, Harry would have asked the Creator what to do.

Teachings

This first case illustrates several things:

  1. Your internal Spirit is in control of your healing, not your mind.

Divine Love Self Healing

2. Your internal Spirit uses the At Oneness Petition to clear layers to *align* you with the Creator at a pace that is safe for you.

3 Your internal Spirit then utilizes the Lovingness Petition to *clear* the layers of energy that cause your symptom, at a pace that is safe for you.

4. The healing of significant illness should be confirmed by a medical physician via testing and/or examination.

5. And yes, the healing can happen this fast!

Harry *totally committed himself* to do what was needed to accomplish his healing. In this case Harry's illness had a *physical* cause: He had previously been exposed to nuclear radiation. Had Harry's tumor been caused by a combination of physical *and* emotional bad energy, his recovery time might have been different.

Harry could not make a direct connection to the Creator when he first started to use the Petition pair. His ability to connect occurred about the third day of Petition use.

If you can make a direct connection before you

Healing a Single Symptom

start the Petitions, it is to your advantage because the Creator will give you exact guidance on the correct symptom to use and guidance when your healing is complete. This will save you time. Otherwise, you can follow the Simplified Protocol given in this book.

There are several other things for you to think about from studying this first Case. If you have undergone any kind of treatment that has weakened your immune system, it may take longer for your body to recover because the immune system and damaged cells also need to be healed.

Further, if you have an emotional cause for your illness, it should be evident that you need to examine how your behavior and thoughts contributed to the problem. Here is some additional information:

1. You can do your At Oneness Healing System in addition to conventional medicine. The choice is entirely yours.

2. I am not dispensing medical treatment, not offering medical advice, not practicing medicine, and am not directly involved with your healing; *you alone* are responsible for your actions and for your success. Your success is between you and the Creator.

Divine Love Self Healing

3. Some individuals experience an "aha moment," getting an intuitive under-standing of what caused their problems and how to avoid similar circumstances in the future.

4. Jobs, activities, and/or relationships: one or more of these may need to change. The point is, if behavior is not modified, other health conditions may manifest.

Chapter 10

Healing Multiple Illnesses

Sally had heart disease and rheumatoid arthritis (RA). She is 50 years old and overweight for her height. She was conflicted because of the pain, fear, and uncertainty surrounding her future. She was spiritual, but did not consider herself religious.

Sally's husband, who had died five years earlier, had not been especially loving to her. She worked in a factory doing repetitive assembly work, until she could no longer flex her fingers due to the arthritis. When she could no longer work and make ends meet, her home went into foreclosure; she moved to an apartment that was smaller and less comfortable than her home. Sally had few friends and did not feel well enough to be social.

Sally was in a bind: Since she could not work a normal job, she did not have enough money for heart surgery. However, if she did not have a heart operation, she faced early death.

It is not uncommon for people like Sally to have difficulty deciding what symptom to correct first. People often feel helpless when confronted with situations that do not appear to have solutions.

Sally was unaware that her *heart condition* had an *emotional* cause but her *arthritis* had both *emotional* and *physical* energy causes. Since the heart condition was life-threatening, it follows that the symptom associated with the heart should be dealt with first.

Sally's heart condition existed on many layers and her rheumatoid arthritis (RA) existed on even more layers. Now let us see how the At Oneness Healing System worked in this case.

In March 2016, Sally attended an At Oneness Healing System webinar where she learned how to apply the Lovingness Petition for correcting both a *physical* symptom and related *emotional* energy at the same time. Sally decided to work on her heart with the At Oneness Healing System Petition pair and the new Simplified Protocol.

In working privately with people who had difficult cases, I learned that faster results were obtained when they used the following phrase to stay connected to Divine Love: "With my Spirit, I accept Divine Love throughout my entire system." Sally used this in her Simplified Protocol.

Day One

Sally said the At Oneness Petition, pulsed her breath, and waited five minutes. During that time, Sally's Spirit *aligned* her through several energy layers, although Sally had no awareness of this. Sally said the Lovingness Petition to remove both physical and unloving energy causes compromising her heart, then pulsed her breath. The Petition Sally used was: "With my Spirit and Divine Love, I focus on all the causes of my heart disease and all the causes of unlovingness towards myself, creation and the Creator. I release all causes to the Creator and ask that the condition be healed according to Divine will."

As Sally waited five minutes, she noticed warmth circulating through her chest. Sally then said, "With my Spirit, I accept Divine Love," and pulsed her breath. Then she set her cell phone countdown timer to 15 minutes and went for a slow walk. Each time the alarm sounded, Sally repeated:

"With my Spirit, I accept Divine Love throughout my entire system," pulsed her breath, and reset the timer. Because Sally continued to stay connected to Divine Love, her Spirit was able to clear bad energy from several layers!

Sally was now healed completely through several layers. Sally noticed that her hands did not hurt so much, but they were still stiff. Her heart continued to feel heavy, with some tightness in her chest. At about 2:00 pm Sally's older sister came for a visit.

Sally took the next five hours off to visit with her sister. Fortunately, Sally and her sister loved each other and they seldom had any disputes, so Sally stayed connected to Divine Love in the interim without doing anything!

At 7:00 pm when her sister left, as Sally closed the door, she noticed less heaviness in her heart and she was breathing easier. In the meantime, her Spirit continued to direct her healing and *aligned* her to the Creator, cleared her physical symptom, and cleared her unlovingness through another layer.

However, while she had done a good job staying connected to Divine Love, there was so much stored *emotional* energy on that new layer that her Spirit could not safely clear it all, so the clearing was only partial.

Healing Multiple Illnesses

Day Two

The next morning Sally decided to play it safe and follow the Simplified Protocol as if she were just beginning. Sally could have just continued to stay "connected," saving herself the extra effort, but she wasn't 100% convinced that the At Oneness Healing System was really working. She thought that perhaps her mind was tricking her into believing that she was getting better.

She said the At Oneness Petition, pulsed her breath, waited 5 minutes, then said the same Lovingness Petition again, pulsed her breath, and waited another 5 minutes. Sally intuitively felt that she was getting better, but physical changes were not obvious.

All day Sally followed the Simplified Protocol, staying connected. By evening, Sally's Spirit and Divine Love had *aligned* her and *healed* her through more layers. Sally was feeling great! Her chest didn't feel tight, she could breathe deeply, and her hands felt better.

Sally didn't realize it but her heart condition was now fully healed!

Day Three

Sally had a busy day planned, so she started

right in by saying "With my Spirit, I accept Divine Love throughout my entire system," and pulsed her breath. She felt a huge rush of energy go through her system! Throughout the day she stayed connected as best she could, even though she missed several of her staying connected Protocol statements.

By nightfall, her Spirit and Divine Love had *aligned* Sally through more energy layers. While Sally had unknowingly cleared the harmful energy from her system that caused her heart condition, she still needed to remove the harmful energy causing rheumatoid arthritis (RA).

Recall that her heart problem was many layers deep but her arthritis was even more layers deep. Therefore, Sally's healing was complete for her heart, but not for her hands. Notice also that the rheumatoid arthritis was apparently *energetically linked* to her heart condition. We know this because Sally was using a symptom of *heart disease*, not a symptom describing her arthritic condition (and yet her hands were improving.)

Day Four

Sally did feel much better. Her blood pressure was 120/60 and her pulse was 60, but her hands still hurt.

Healing Multiple Illnesses

Sally stayed connected during the day and her Spirit and Divine Love healed her through *all* the affected energy layers. Her Spirit did not need to go further because the harmful energy for both complaints had been taken care of. Sally noticed that her hands were fully flexible, with no pain and no swelling. Apparently, Sally's rheumatoid arthritis was healed *without* specifying it as a symptom; this is not unusual. She was ecstatic and rushed to the phone to call her sister with the good news!

Sally knew through her webinar training that she needed to consciously stay connected to Divine Love for three more days, and so she did.

Sally called her doctor on the 8th day after beginning the At Oneness Healing System and got an appointment for the 10th day after she started her Petitions.

On Day 10, she remained joyful. During her appointment, she asked her cardiologist to run tests to prove that she was well. Initially, her doctor was puzzled and not anxious to do this, but he observed that Sally evidenced enough changes to warrant re-testing.

Her doctor was shocked by the test results. Sally reported that the doctor said: "Well something obviously happened. All I can say is that it is a miracle!" Sally was surprised that the doctor did not embrace her wellness with the same joy and enthusiasm that she felt. (Had Sally divulged her experience with the At Oneness Healing System to her doctor, he might have had the opportunity to evaluate how he could use it with his other patients.)

This Case illustrates many principles:

1. It demonstrates how the Petitions work together as a pair and how the Spirit operates in the body for a complex healing.

2. The At Oneness Petition works to clear all the spiritual background energy that may, or may not be directly involved with the symptom to be healed.

3. The Lovingness Petition can remove both *physical* and *unloving* energy. Correcting the rheumatoid arthritis at the same time as the heart was unusual, but I have seen other cases where multiple problems also corrected simultaneously.

4. If Sally's rheumatoid arthritis had not healed, she would have waited a few more days to allow her body to finish healing. Then she could have started a new Simplified Protocol using the phrase

swollen hands and knuckles as her symptom to heal her arthritis.

AOHS Summary of Use

The Simplified Protocol is important to the At Oneness Healing System's Divine Love spiritual healing because it applies order and discipline to keep a person on track. We have learned through experience that if someone uses the Petition pair in the reverse order (Lovingness Petition first and At Oneness Petition second), healing may not take place rapidly enough to provide relief for life-threatening or painful conditions.

The At Oneness Petition operates first. It clears layers of a *spiritual* or *mental* nature (unrelated to the condition to be healed) that interfere with healing (such as subconscious resistance and fear). Once the unrelated interference is cleared out, the Lovingness Petition is able to more effectively move down through those same layers, removing both the *physical* and *emotional* energy associated with the stated symptom.

Notice that the order of symptom healing in the Lovingness Petition is to specify the *physical* symptom first, followed by the *emotional* symptom phrase, ". . . and all the causes of unlovingness towards myself, creation and the

Divine Love Self Healing

Creator." This helps ensure that only the emotional energy associated with a desired physical symptom is removed. Otherwise, Spirit would address all emotional conditions, which could extend healing time.

Also, the Lovingness Petition should not be used alone (except for a pop-up condition). This is because the At Oneness Petition prepares the way.

Still confused?

Think of it this way: In American football, the offensive linemen attempt to push defensive linemen out of the way so that the ball carrier can successfully get through the defense. If the offensive linemen are unable to open that defensive line, the ball carrier is stopped.

The At Oneness Petition is represented by the offensive linemen; the Lovingness Petition is represented by the ball carrier.

As you study the cases, you may wonder if healing always works this fast. The fact is that for some people it works even faster! For others, it may take longer because of the amount of trapped energy to be removed from their layers.

Healing Multiple Illnesses

Some people on our webinars have experienced spontaneous remissions and instantaneous healings. Others take longer, anywhere from hours to days, and some make no progress at all because they are not committed to their wellness.

You have had an inside look at a phenomenal healing system that works! The rest is up to you. Will you be one of the people who write to me of your healing success? I sincerely hope so.